D0734446

JumpStart Your Priorities

Books by Dr. John C. Maxwell
Can Teach You How to Be a REAL Success

Relationships
25 Ways to Win with People
Becoming a Person of Influence
Encouragement Changes Everything
Ethics 101
*Everyone Communicates,
Few Connect*
The Power of Partnership
Relationships 101
Winning With People

Equipping
The 15 Invaluable Laws of Growth
*The 17 Essential Qualities
of a Team Player*
*The 17 Indisputable Laws
of Teamwork*
Developing the Leaders Around You
Equipping 101
Learning from the Giants
JumpStart Your Growth
Make Today Count
Mentoring 101
My Dream Map
Partners in Prayer
Put Your Dream to the Test
Running with the Giants
Talent Is Never Enough
Today Matters
Wisdom from Women in the Bible
Your Road Map for Success

Attitude
Attitude 101
The Difference Maker
Failing Forward
How Successful People Think
How Successful People Win
Intentional Living
JumpStart Your Thinking
*Sometimes You Win,
Sometimes You Learn*
Success 101
Thinking for a Change
The Winning Attitude

Leadership
*The 10th Anniversary Edition
of The 21 Irrefutable Laws
of Leadership*
*The 21 Indispensable Qualities
of a Leader*
*The 21 Most Powerful Minutes
in a Leader's Day*
The 360 Degree Leader
Developing the Leader Within You
The 5 Levels of Leadership
Go for Gold
Good Leaders Ask Great Questions
JumpStart Your Leadership
Leadership 101
Leadership Gold
*Leadership Promises for
Every Day*
*What Successful People Know
About Leadership*

A 90-DAY
IMPROVEMENT
PLAN

JumpStart Your Priorities

JOHN C. MAXWELL

CENTER
STREET

NEW YORK BOSTON NASHVILLE

Copyright © 2016 by John C. Maxwell

All rights reserved. All rights reserved. In accordance with the U.S. Copyright Act of 1976, the scanning, uploading, and electronic sharing of any part of this book without the permission of the publisher is unlawful piracy and theft of the author's intellectual property. If you would like to use material from the book (other than for review purposes), prior written permission must be obtained by contacting the publisher at permissions@hbgusa. com. Thank you for your support of the author's rights.

The author is represented by Yates & Yates, LLP, Literary Agency, Orange, California.

Literary development and design: Koechel Peterson & Associates, Inc., Minneapolis, Minnesota.

This book has been adapted from *Today Matters*, copyright © 2004 by John C. Maxwell. Published by Center Street.

Center Street
Hachette Book Group
237 Park Avenue
New York, NY 10017

www.CenterStreet.com

Printed in the United States of America

RRD-C

First trade edition: August 2016

10 9 8 7 6 5 4 3 2 1

Center Street is a division of Hachette Book Group, Inc.

The Center Street name and logo are trademarks of Hachette Book Group, Inc.

The Hachette Speakers Bureau provides a wide range of authors for speaking events. To find out more, go to www.hachettespeakersbureau.com or call (866) 376-6591.

The publisher is not responsible for websites (or their content) that are not owned by the publisher.

ISBN 978-1-4555-8836-7

*I*NTRODUCTION

*H*ow would you describe your life? Are you achieving what you desire? Are you accomplishing the things that are important to you? How do your prospects look for the future?

Everyone wants to be successful and fulfilled, but most people cannot define what success means to them, and even fewer people understand how the way they live today impacts their tomorrow. Why is that? The root of the problem is that most people misunderstand success, thinking it a mystical something that just happens, or that it comes from being lucky or working hard or making connections.

Here's the missing piece: *The secret of your success is determined by your daily agenda.* It all comes down to what you do today. You see, success doesn't just suddenly occur one day. For that matter, neither does failure. Each is a process. Every day of your life is merely preparation for the next. What you become is the result of what you do today.

Growth, success, and fulfillment come from making wise decisions on the priorities for your life and then managing them well in your daily agenda. You begin to build a better life by determining to make good decisions, but that alone is not enough. You need to know what priorities to set for your life. I've given the subject a lot of thought, talked to many successful people, and narrowed down the list of critical life priorities for success to twelve. I call them the "Daily Dozen":

1. Attitude: Choose and display the right attitudes daily.

2. Focus: Think and act with focus daily.

3. Health: Know and follow healthy guidelines daily.

4. Family: Communicate with and care for my family daily.

5. Thinking: Practice and develop good thinking daily.

6. Commitment: Make and keep proper commitments daily.

7. Finances: Make and properly manage dollars daily.

8. Faith: Deepen and live out my faith daily.

9. Relationships: Initiate and invest in solid relationships daily.

10. Generosity: Plan for and model generosity daily.

11. Values: Embrace and practice good values daily.

12. Growth: Seek and experience improvements daily.

Please don't let the length of the list bother you. What I'm suggesting is that if you make decisions in those key areas once and for all—and then manage those decisions daily—you can create the kind of tomorrow you desire. *Successful people make the right priority decisions early and manage those decisions daily.* The earlier you make those decisions and the longer you manage them, the more successful you can become.

Most people can make good decisions once they know what their priorities should be. But character and perseverance determine what happens after the decision is made. To help you follow through in each critical area, I've recommended disciplines for you to practice for the next ninety days so that you can establish your personal priorities and manage your decisions well in your life. You will be provided with clear steps to help you tackle each of the twelve priorities and make it a success asset. Just focus on one area at a time to make the greatest progress. And remember, when it comes to the big decisions in life, once you make them, you won't have to keep dealing with them in that way again.

What will it take for you to jumpstart your priorities? Consistently set aside 15 minutes every day for the next 90 days to think intentionally about your priorities and how you manage them in your daily agenda. Read and consider the inspirational quote for the day, read and digest the lesson, and move forward by taking action in response to the question.

If you spend time implementing the kind of priorities described in the daily readings for the next three months, you will place yourself on the pathway of success. It could be the difference that makes all the difference in your life!

Ready? Let's get started!

DAY

1

The winner's edge is not in a gifted birth, a high IQ, or in talent. The winner's edge is all in the attitude, not aptitude. Attitude is the criterion for success. But you can't buy an attitude for a million dollars. Attitudes are not for sale.

DENIS WAITLEY

While it is possible for people with great talent or drive to achieve some degree of success with a bad attitude, it doesn't happen very often and it doesn't make them happy. On the other hand, even barely average people can do great things when their attitudes are great and give them a winner's perspective. Your attitude toward a task affects its outcome more than anything else, and your attitude toward others often determines their attitude toward you. And it is your attitude, not your achievements, that gives you happiness and is contagious in its positive impact on others.

Many people mistakenly believe their attitude is set and can't be changed. But that's not true. Your attitude is a choice, and you need to have a great attitude because it gives you possibilities.

The first Daily Dozen priority you need to focus on is this: *I am going to keep a positive attitude and use it to influence others.*

Describe how you assess your attitude today. Write a declaration of commitment to keep a positive attitude and use it to influence others, then sign and date it.

DAY

2

*What lies behind us and what lies before us are tiny
matters compared to what lies within us.*
WALT EMERSON

After my wife, Margaret, and I had been married
for four or five years, we were at a conference for pas-
tors where a woman asked Margaret, "Does John make
you happy?" I have to say, I was really looking forward to
hearing her answer. I'm an attentive husband, and I love
Margaret dearly. What kind of praise would she lavish on
me?

I was taken aback when she responded, "No, he
doesn't." Fortunately, she continued, "The first two or
three years we were married, I thought it was John's job
to make me happy. But he didn't, even though he's a good
husband. Nobody can make another person happy. That
is my job."

As a young newlywed, she figured out something
some people never learn. Each of us must *take responsibility for our own attitudes.* You make it your priority when
you take charge of the way you look at life. Everybody has
at least a few areas in their thinking and some attitudes
that need to change. If you want to improve your life, you
need to go after those areas.

Make a list of your negative attitudes and habits or ones you want to improve. Next to each one, write the positive response that you will take responsibility for.

DAY

3

*Things turn out best for the people who make
the best of the way things turn out.*
JOHN WOODEN

If you desire to change yourself, start with your mind. Believe you can improve, that you can change into the person you desire to be. If your attitude changes, everything else can follow. When you see yourself as you could be, you can learn to acquire the skills of, and act, talk, and conduct yourself like the person you want to become. The transformation will come, even though it often may seem barely noticeable; it just requires patience.

So, if you are one of the many people who finds fault and complains about many things, make it your priority to *develop a high appreciation for life.* Appreciation isn't a matter of taste or sophistication; it's a matter of perspective. The place to start a positive attitude is with the little things. If you can learn to appreciate them and be grateful for them, you'll appreciate the big things as well as everything in between.

List three areas of your thinking that you will purposefully start thinking positively about today. Write down a goal of the number of times to do it for each one and keep track of it throughout the day.

DAY

4

*People don't really care how much you know
until they know how much you care.*
THEODORE ROOSEVELT

One of the secrets of maintaining a good attitude is valuing people. You can't dislike people and have a good attitude at the same time.

Think about it: Have you ever met anyone who always treated people badly but had a positive attitude? Likewise, you cannot have a bad attitude and encourage others at the same time. Encouraging others means helping people, looking for the best in them, and trying to bring out their positive qualities. That process drives negative thoughts right out of your head.

Your interaction with others sets the tone of your day. It's like the music of your life. When your interaction with others is poor, it's like having to listen to cacophonous music. But when you *place a high value on people* and you treat them well, it's like listening to a sweet melody as you go through your day.

What positive actions or expressions can you take to encourage and build up at least three people today? Write them down, then follow through on them and return here and record how it affected your own attitude.

DAY

5

Our attitudes control our lives. Attitudes are a secret power working twenty-four hours a day, for good or bad. It is of paramount importance that we know how to harness and control this great force.

CHARLES SIMMONS

To benefit from the possibilities of a positive attitude, you need to do more than just make the decision to be positive. You also have to manage that decision. For me, it means setting this priority: *Every day I will make the adjustments necessary to keep my attitude right.* If this is new territory for you, you may be wondering how to do it.

First, *recognize that your attitude does not naturally or easily stay positive.* For example, a lifelong attitude weakness I've had is my impatience with people, and I still battle it. Every day I ask myself, "Have I been impatient with someone?" When I have, I apologize to the person. I've had to do that more times than I'd like to admit.

Like any discipline, your attitude will not take care of itself. That's why it needs to be a priority attended to daily. The stronger your natural inclination to be pessimistic or critical, the more attention your attitude will need. Begin each day with an attitude check. And watch for red flags signaling that your attitude might be in trouble.

Find four attitude quotes or positive sayings and write them down here. Then write them on individual sheets of paper and place them in places where you will see them several times a day—next to your computer, on your bathroom mirror, in your daily planner, etc.

DAY

6

To succeed, you need to find something to hold on to, something to motivate you, something to inspire you.
TONY DORSETT

If you want to maintain a positive attitude every day, make it a priority to *find something positive in everything*. It may not always be easy, but even in the midst of difficult situations you can find something good. When Mother Teresa was asked the requirements for people assisting in her work with the destitute in Calcutta, she cited two things: the desire to work hard and a joyful attitude. If someone could be expected to be joyful among the dying and the poorest of the poor, we can do the same in our situation.

Then take that attitude another step: *find someone positive in every situation*. Nothing helps you to remain positive like having an ally. The world is filled with negative and positive people. When you find positive ones, seek them out. If you're having a hard time, get close and "draft" behind them the way racers do. If they're having difficulty, you be the one to go out front and make things easier. Two positive people are much better at fighting off the blues than someone going it alone.

Describe two attitudes that are a requirement for you to be successful in your situation. Also, write the name of a positive person in your situation and what you will do today to become a closer ally with him or her.

DAY

7

There is little difference in people, but that little difference makes a big difference. The little difference is attitude. The big difference is whether it is positive or negative.

W. CLEMENT STONE

My father retired in his mid-seventies, having spent his entire life in public speaking. He came from a modest background, so he was always working hard to learn and grow. When I was a kid, he used to pay my brother, Larry, and me ten cents for every grammar mistake we found him making when he was preaching. It was just one example of the priority he placed upon constantly trying to improve himself. (I suspect he also did it so that we would learn more about grammar ourselves.)

You can do a similar kind of thing when it comes to your attitude. You—or someone you enlist—can *be on the lookout for negative words* in your vocabulary so that you can eliminate and replace them. Here's a list to get you started: I can't/I can; If only/I will; I don't think/I know; I don't have the time/I will make the time; maybe/absolutely; I'm afraid/I'm confident; I don't believe/I'm sure.

If you continually look for and embrace the positive and eliminate the negative, you'll help yourself to begin thinking more positively every day.

Spend some time reflecting on the negative words that you think and speak. List them as well as the positive words you will embrace today. As you discover more words in future days, return here and list them for elimination.

DAY

8

When we learn to give thanks, we are learning
to concentrate not on the bad things,
but on the good things in our lives.

AMY VANDERBILT

If you want to maintain a positive attitude, make it a priority to *say something positive in every conversation.* For me, it starts with those closest to me. When my wife looks beautiful (which is often!), I tell her so. I compliment my children and absolutely pour out positive praise on my grandchildren every time I see them. But I don't stop there. I sincerely compliment, praise, acknowledge, bolster, encourage, and reward people whenever I can. It's wonderful for me as well as for others. I know you can learn to do it too.

Also make it a priority to *express gratitude to others daily.* Of all the virtues, gratitude seems to be the least expressed today. How often do you go out of your way to extend your thanks to others? I recommend you keep a gratitude journal to help you appreciate life. Thinking about the good things and remaining grateful helps us to have a more positive attitude. And having a positive attitude prompts us to think about the good rather than the bad. It's a positive cycle that helps to fuel itself.

Write down the names of at least three people and the expressions of gratitude that you will share with them today. After you've thanked those people, write down how it affected your attitude.

DAY

9

*The reason most goals are not achieved is that
we spend our time doing second things first.*
ROBERT J. MCKAIN

When I began my career, most of my time was spent in doing counseling and administration—neither of which goes with my natural gifts or inclinations. I was neither fulfilled nor effective until I came across an idea about prioritizing your life called the Pareto Principle. It said that by focusing your attention on the top 20 percent of all your priorities, you would get an 80 percent return on your effort. That was my Eureka moment! That's when I made this life decision: *I will give focus and energy in my life to those things that give the highest return.*

No Daily Dozen priority has added more to my success than this principle. Your focus determines how you spend your time, and time is precious. To be successful, you can't just run on the fast track; you have to run on your track. I realized that I needed to focus 80 percent of my time, energy, and resources on my areas of strength, not on counseling and administration. People who reach their potential and fulfill their dreams determine and act on the right focus daily. Excellence comes from doing the right things right.

Describe how you have prioritized your life up until now. What do you need to do to improve that? Write a declaration to determine and act on important priorities daily, then sign and date it.

....

....

....

....

....

....

....

....

....

....

....

....

....

....

....

....

....

DAY

10

*The art of being wise is the art of
knowing what to overlook.*
WILLIAM JAMES

When I discovered that I needed to prioritize my life, I started by asking myself three critical questions to establish my focus:

1. What is *required* of me? Any realistic assessment of priorities in any area of life must start with an evaluation of what a person *must* do. For you to be a good spouse or parent or employee, what is required of you? When deciding what to focus on, always start with and give careful thought to the requirement question.

2. What gives me the greatest *return*? As you progress in your career, you discover that some activities yield a much higher return for the effort than others do. Focus your attention on those high-return activities.

3. What gives me the greatest *reward*? If you do only what you must and what is effective, you will be highly productive, but you may not be content. You must first possess the discipline to take care of the first two areas, but it's also important to consider what gives you personal satisfaction. Some people want to start with the reward question and go no further than that.

Answer the three critical questions in the context of your personal and your professional life.

DAY

11

He is a wise man who wastes no energy on pursuits for which he is not fitted; and he is wiser still who from among the things he can do well, chooses and resolutely follows the best.
WILLIAM GLADSTONE

To *stay in your strength zone* is a priority that will increase your productivity and ability to reach your potential. To get a good handle on your strengths, explore some of these suggestions:

Trial and Error: Nothing teaches you more than your successes and failures. Any time something seems to be all "trial," it's probably time to move on. But you've got to take the risk of making mistakes and failing to find your successes.

The Counsel of Others: Asking others to evaluate your effectiveness is not always fun, but it is always helpful. Choose people whose only agenda is to help you.

Personality Tests: Evaluations, such as DISC, Florence Littauer's Personality Profile, and Myers-Briggs, can help to clarify some of your natural inclinations and to reveal some strengths and weaknesses you aren't aware of.

Personal Experience: You really get a feel for how well you do something by doing it repeatedly. Remember this: Experience isn't always the best teacher—evaluated experience is!

Describe what you think your strength zone is. What successes and failures have you had that corroborate that? List two people whom you will ask to evaluate your effectiveness and write down how they respond.

....

....

....

....

....

....

....

....

....

....

....

....

....

....

....

....

....

....

....

DAY

12

The key is not to prioritize what's on your schedule,
but to schedule your priorities.

STEPHEN COVEY

One of the things I noticed after making my focus decision was that priorities shift very easily. For that reason they must be continually evaluated and guarded. My reminder to manage the discipline of focus is this: *Every day I will make sure I am focusing on the right things.*

Priorities don't stay put; you have to revisit and evaluate them every day. Why? Because conditions continually change. So do methods of getting things done. Your values, once defined, are going to be steady. You will be able to rely on them. But how you carry them out needs to be flexible. Over the next four days, we'll explore how to do this.

*Evaluate a task
that you have
today—describe
how you will
get it done,
when you will
do it, and how
you will follow
through on your
plan and how
you will measure
your results.*

DAY

13

The older I get the more wisdom I find in the ancient rule of taking first things first—a process that often reduces the most complex human problem to a manageable proportion.

DWIGHT D. EISENHOWER

If you are going to live your life focusing your attention on the right things, you must *plan your time carefully*. Here's one effective way:

Charles Schwab, president of Bethlehem Steel, met with management consultant Ivy Lee because he wanted to improve his company's productivity. Lee handed Schwab a blank sheet of paper and said, "Write down the six most important things you have to do tomorrow, then number them in the order of their importance." Schwab complied. Lee continued, "First thing tomorrow morning start working on item number one, just number one, and stay with it until it's completed. Then take item number two the same way. Don't worry if you have finished only one or two by day's end. You'll be working on the most important ones. . . . Do this every workday. After you're convinced of the value of this system, have your people try it out."

Schwab said it was the most profitable lesson he had ever learned. Not long after that, Bethlehem Steel became the largest independent steel producer of its day.

Utilizing Lee's plan on how to use your time today, list the six most important things you have to do, then do them one at a time according to importance, even if it takes longer than a day. After you complete all six, describe the impact on your efficiency.

DAY

14

*Things that matter most must never be at the
mercy of things that matter least.*
JOHANN WOLFGANG VON GOETHE

I don't mean to insult your intelligence by suggesting that you *follow your plan,* but it needs to be said if you are going to manage the discipline of focus every day. According to time management expert Alec Mackenzie, surveys show that most executives don't get to their most important tasks until midafternoon. Why? Most finished off low-priority tasks so that they could have a sense of accomplishment. If you refocus your attention and plan your day but don't follow through, your results will be the same as those of someone who didn't focus at all.

Remember: Your greatest possession is the twenty-four hours you have directly ahead of you. How will you spend them? Will you focus on priorities or allow pointless e-mails, unimportant tasks, telemarketers, interruptions, and other distractions to consume your day? Will you take complete responsibility for how you spend your time, take control of the things you can, and make today yours by following through on your plan? If you don't take control of your time today, someone or something else will take it.

Name one important matter that you are procrastinating on and write a declaration of the specific steps you will take today to follow through with your plan.

DAY

*No executive has ever suffered because his
subordinates were strong and effective.*

PETER DRUCKER

If you are going to manage the discipline of focus every day, *delegate whenever possible.*

How do you find the right standard for delegation? When is it right to hand something off or hold on to it? Here's my guideline: If someone else can do a task I'm doing 80 percent as well as I do, I hand it off. That's pretty good. And if I do a good job of motivating, encouraging, and rewarding them, they will only get better. I've handed off responsibilities using that standard, and after a while, the person who's taken on the job has gone on to do it much better than I could. That is very rewarding.

Today I am surrounded by people on my team who do things much better than I can. They make up the difference in my weak areas and exceed my expectations in others. They lift me to a level higher than I could ever attain myself, and they allow me to live out my priorities.

Write down three tasks that you will release to others whom you think are ready for the responsibilities and record the results.

....

....

....

....

....

....

....

....

....

....

....

....

....

....

....

....

....

....

DAY

The key is in not spending time, but in investing it.
STEPHEN R. COVEY

There's one more area I want to address regarding managing your focus, and that's the need to *prioritize how you spend time with people.* Waylon Moore has observed that often "we spend priority time with problem people when we should be spending it with potential people." That's true.

How do you decide whom to spend time with? Here's what I use to evaluate where to invest my time:

- Value to the team
- Natural ability
- Responsibility
- Timing
- Potential
- Mentoring fit

Certainly, you want to treat everyone with respect and try to have a good, positive relationship with everyone. But you should not spend time with everyone equally.

Write a
description of
how you are
prioritizing
your time with
people, the
challenges you
face, and what
you can do to
improve that.

DAY

17

*If you had a million-dollar racehorse, would you allow it
to smoke cigarettes, drink whiskey, and stay out all night?
How about a thousand-dollar dog?*

ZIG ZIGLAR

At the age of fifty-one, I made this Daily Dozen priority that regards my health: *I will take good care of myself by exercising and eating right.* I did so after the evening of December 18, 1998, when I suffered a serious heart attack and only survived because the doctor performed a newly developed procedure. If I'd had my heart attack a year earlier, it would have killed me! I hope you will make health your priority rather than take your good health for granted, work too hard, and not exercise enough, as I did, and face what I faced.

If you know the value of good health, yet you've had a hard time making the commitment to know and follow healthy guidelines, I have some suggestions to help you make it a priority. The first is to *have a purpose worth living for.* A sense of purpose helps a person to make a decision to change and then to follow through with the discipline required to make that change permanent. When a friend was surprised to see me pass on desserts after my heart attack, my response was simple: "My craving for life is greater."

Where do you stand today on the priority of health? Write a list of all the things and people whom you have to live for. Then write the benefits that will come from having a long and healthy life.

DAY

18

*The problem with the rat race is that even
if you win, you're still a rat.*

LILY TOMLIN

Another suggestion to help you make health a priority is to *do work you enjoy*. One of the greatest causes of debilitating stress in people's lives is doing jobs they don't enjoy. One major frustration that contributes to that stress is doing work you don't think is important. If you do work that you believe adds no value to yourself or to others, you quickly become demoralized and it will wear you down. To remain healthy, your work must be in alignment with your values.

Another reason some people don't like their work is because they do jobs that keep them in an area of weakness. Nobody can do that long and succeed. One of the ways you can tell you're working in an area of strength is that it actually gives you energy. Even if you're in the early stages of your career and you're not very good at something you're doing, you can still tell it's an area of strength by paying attention to how you respond to your failures. Mistakes that challenge you show your areas of strength. Mistakes that threaten you show your areas of weakness.

Describe whether you are doing work you love. Does your career make the best use of your natural abilities, skills, and interests? Do you need to make changes to get your work aligned with your life purpose? How will you do that?

DAY

If I had known I was going to live this long,
I would have taken better care of myself.
MICKEY MANTLE

I think that Mantle's statement could apply to most people as they age. Part of taking care of yourself and making your health a daily priority includes *finding and maintaining the pace that's right* for you. If you take life more slowly than your energy level is capable of, you can become lazy. If you continually run at a pace faster than you are capable, as I did, you can burn out. You need to find your balance. I'm constantly trying to strike a balance between my desire to maintain a healthy pace of life and my drive to accomplish all I can during my lifetime.

Another suggestion that I've found helpful is that we should never take life or ourselves too seriously. Each of us has idiosyncrasies that can cause us to either despair or to laugh. For example, when it comes to anything related to tools, I'm Mr. Hopeless. I don't let that bother me at all. If you can *laugh at yourself loudly and often*, you will find it liberating. There's no better way to prevent stress from becoming distress.

Write an assessment of the pace at which you are running your life. What steps can you take today to bring it into the right balance?

DAY

20

An individual's self-concept affects every aspect of human behavior. The ability to learn . . . the capacity to grow and change . . . the choice of friends, mates, and careers. It is no exaggeration to say that a strong positive self-image is the best possible preparation for success in life.

JOYCE BROTHERS

Irving Berlin, creator of innumerable popular and Broadway hits such as "White Christmas" and "Easter Parade" and songs such as "God Bless America," was once asked in an interview whether there was a question he wished someone would have asked him. Berlin replied, "Yes, there is one. 'What do you think of the many songs you've written that didn't become hits?' My reply would be that I still think they are wonderful!"

Berlin had a *good sense of self-worth* and confidence in his work, regardless of whether it was accepted by others. That's certainly not true of everyone. In fact, a poor or distorted self-image is the cause of many health-threatening conditions and activities, from drug use and alcoholism to eating disorders and obesity. If your self-image is driving you to do things that negatively impact your health, seek help.

How is your sense of self-worth and confidence affecting your health and behavior? What steps, both today and in the future, can you take to improve that?

DAY

21

*The only way to keep your health is to eat what
you don't want, drink what you don't like,
and do what you'd rather not.*
MARK TWAIN

For some people, the disciplines of health appear to
be easy, but I possess a "foodaholic" bent that has made it
a constant battle. Nevertheless, following my heart attack,
I had a new discipline to manage: *Every day I will eat low-
fat foods and exercise for at least thirty-five minutes.* I was
told that eighty-five percent of all heart patients quit their
healthy regimen within six months. Even though I had
not succeeded in this area my first fifty years, I was determined to succeed in it the rest of my life.

As I fight the good fight, I hope you'll join me by
making it your priority to *eat right.* The key to healthy
eating is moderation and managing what you eat every
day. Don't rely on crash diets. Don't worry about what
you ate yesterday. Don't put off good eating until tomorrow. Just try to eat what's best for you in the moment.
Focus on now. And if you're not sure how you're doing or
what you should (and shouldn't) be eating, get a physical.
Your doctor will let you know how you're doing and how
to change your diet.

Describe where your priority to eat right stands today. What foods do you need to reduce or eliminate and what foods do you need to add? Make an appointment with your doctor to discuss your overall health and physical condition. After you have met, write down his or her assessment.

DAY

22

Being physically fit is a way of protecting yourself against coronary heart disease, hypertension and stroke, plus adult-onset diabetes, obesity, osteoporosis, probably colon cancer and maybe other cancers, and probably clinical depression. Exercise has an enormous impact on the quality of life.

DR. RALPH S. PAFFENBERGER JR.

Most people I know either love exercise and do it excessively or they hate it and avoid it completely; yet *consistent exercise is one of the keys to good health.* One of the tough things about exercising is that the immediate payoff seems so small. You weigh yourself after exercising. Nothing. You exercise the next day and the next. Still nothing. Then after the fifth day of exercise, maybe you see that you've lost half a pound. It's easy to get discouraged. But your four days of discipline make the progress you see on the fifth day possible.

The key to success in this area is consistency. I exercise a minimum of five days a week by swimming for at least thirty-five minutes a day. That's what my doctor has recommended. If you don't already practice the daily habit of exercise, find a way to get started. It doesn't really matter what you do as long as you do it. Talk to your doctor. Sign up for a class at a gym. Do whatever it takes to begin a regimen that's right for you.

Describe where your priority to exercise stands today. What type of exercise do you enjoy? What can you do today to get yourself into a regimen that's right for you?

DAY

23

When you're dealing with stress, the problem may not be the stressful situation as much as the effort to avoid that situation and the feelings it arouses.

TED A. GROSSBART

A hundred years ago, most causes of illness were related to infectious disease. Today, they are related to stress. Everybody faces problems and feels pressure at times. Whether or not that pressure becomes stress depends on *how you handle it*. Here's how I handle issues to keep them from becoming stressful to me:

- Family problems: communication, unconditional love, time together
- Limited options: creative thinking, advice from others, tenacity
- Staff productivity problems: immediate confrontation with the person and addressing the issue
- Staff leaders with bad attitudes: removal

I've found that the worst thing I can do when it comes to any kind of potential pressure situation is to put off dealing with it. If you address problems with people as quickly as possible and don't let issues build up, you greatly reduce the chances of being stressed out.

How would you assess your ability to handle stress? Describe one issue that you have put off dealing with as well as the specific steps you will take today to begin to resolve it.

DAY

24

*I never think of age. I think about today.
I don't think about tomorrow. I think about
this moment and what I am going to do.*
JACK LALANNE

Perhaps you have fallen short, as I did, in making health a priority and feel it's too late for you. Please don't be discouraged. Though you cannot go back and make a brand-new start, you can start now and make a brand-new end.

Any time I'm feeling discouraged, I think about fitness expert Jack LaLanne, who lived to be over ninety-six years old and never allowed age to overcome his desire to know and follow healthy guidelines daily. He made his health decision when he was just fifteen, changing his eating habits and beginning to work out. His exercise program was on television from 1951 to 1985—decades before health and fitness really began being promoted. His advice is that anyone at any age in any health situation can become more healthy: "If they're overweight, normalize that weight. Quit exceeding the feed limit. And exercise is number one! I don't care what you have wrong with you, you can do something—right? Maybe there are ten exercises you can't do, but there are a hundred you can do."

Having reflected on your health over the past days, write out a declaration of your decision to make health one of your priorities. Describe what the compounding benefits will be.

DAY

25

When you have a strong family life, you receive the message that you are loved, cared for, and important. The positive intake of love, affection, and respect . . . gives you inner resources to deal with life more successfully.

Nick Stinnet

There's no doubt that the relationships you have with members of your immediate family and with your spouse are the most important ones in your life. The people closest to you form you—and are formed by you.

In 1986, about the same time my career was taking off, the marriages of some of my colleagues and friends were falling apart. That really got my attention. I wanted to be successful, but I didn't want to lose my family in the process. That prompted me to make one of my Daily Dozen life decisions and to rewrite my definition of success. From that moment, *success meant having those closest to me love and respect me the most.* Success would be impossible if I achieved outwardly but failed to take my family with me on the journey. Caring for and communicating with my family became one of my life's priorities.

I hope you will make this a priority for yourself as well. No matter what your situation is, you can benefit from the stability that comes from communicating with and caring for your family daily.

Where do you stand as regards the priority you've made of your family? Write a declaration of what you want it to be, sign it, and date it.

DAY

26

Before going to War—pray once.
Before going to Sea—pray twice.
Before getting Married—pray three times.
RUSSIAN PROVERB

To make your family one of your life priorities requires that you first *determine your priorities*. I began learning this lesson the hard way after getting married to Margaret and starting my first career job within a month. I gave my job everything I had, working a six-day workweek as well as my day off. I was neglecting Margaret and our marriage, and a marriage can't survive forever on leftovers. It needs to be fed continually, or it will eventually starve, and there are grim statistics for what occurs when you let that happen.

Building a solid family doesn't just happen on its own. You have to work at it. After I got the message that I was neglecting Margaret, I changed my approach to my career. I carved out time for her. I protected my day off. And we dedicated money in our budget to facilitate special times together. I still wanted to be successful, but not at the cost of my family! And I'm still working on making my family a priority. Anyone who neglects or abandons his or her family for fame, status, or financial gain isn't really successful.

How much time do you give to your family daily? Talk to the members of your family and ask them to give you their honest assessment. What changes do you need to make?

DAY

27

To us, family means putting your arms
around each other and being there.

BARBARA BUSH

Once you've determined to make your family a priority, you have to decide what you want your family to stand for. That should be based on your values. In the first decade of our marriage, Margaret and I decided on our *personal philosophy of family*. First, we tried to live it out as a couple. Then when we had children, we worked to make it the foundation of our choices as parents. For us, the bottom line on family was for us to cultivate and maintain our commitment to God, our continual personal growth, our common experiences, our confidence in God, ourselves, and others, and our contributions to life.

This is our list. I'm not suggesting that you adopt our philosophy regarding family. I know you will want to create your own. Here's my suggestion: Keep it simple. If you come up with a list of seventeen things you want to live out, you won't be able to do it. You may not even be able to remember it! Whittle the list down to the nonnegotiables.

Dedicate some time to articulating your philosophy of family. If you are married, spend time with your spouse talking about it. What are your nonnegotiables? Write them down, recognizing they will evolve over time.

....

....

....

....

....

....

....

....

....

....

....

....

....

....

....

....

....

....

....

DAY

28

Many marriages would be better if the husband and the wife clearly understood that they are on the same side.
ZIG ZIGLAR

I think a lot of people go into marriage expecting it to be easy. Maybe they've seen too many movies. Marriage isn't easy. Family isn't easy. Life isn't easy. Expect problems, stay committed, and *develop a strategy for getting through the rough times.* Some people call family meetings to discuss issues. Others create systems or rules. We have friends who developed a system of fair fight rules after they had been married a few years, and their system has worked great for them for well over twenty years.

Think about how you could improve your problem solving at home. Talk to your family members about it (during a calm time, not in the middle of a conflict). Use whatever kind of problem-solving strategy works for you. Just be sure that it fosters and promotes three things: (1) better understanding; (2) positive change; and (3) growing relationships.

What strategies do you have in place to get your family through the rough times? What will you do today to improve your problem solving at home?

DAY

29

Family is not an important thing; it's everything.
MICHAEL J. FOX

The desire to make your family a priority is one thing; actually living it out is something else. I found that it's often easier to get the approval of strangers and colleagues than it is to get respect from those who know you best. So I practice this discipline: *Every day I work hard on gaining the love and respect of those closest to me.*

If you desire to strengthen your family life and make it a source of stability, try practicing some of the priorities that I'll share here and over the next three days. My first suggestion is to *put your family on your calendar first.* Work, hobbies, and interests will gobble up every bit of your time if you let them. If you don't create boundaries for how you spend your time, your family will always get the leftovers.

Here's a wise perspective on it: Never let yourself feel that you ought to be at work when you're with your family, and vice versa. If you and your family can figure out and agree on how much time you should spend together and you protect those times, you should be able to adopt that mind-set.

Review your calendar and consider it in the light of the priority of your family. What can you do to build in more time for your family members? What dates can you add, and what dates do you need to guard as family days?

DAY

30

I have the best memories as a kid eating ice cream. It was a family tradition that I had with my father. It was nice.
MICHAEL STRAHAN

To help you make your family a priority, I strongly recommend that you *create and maintain family traditions.* Here's why: What makes families happy isn't receiving things; it's doing things together.

Traditions give your family a shared history and a strong sense of identity. Don't you remember how your family celebrated Thanksgiving as a child? How about Christmas? (And didn't you think yours was the right way when you got married and your spouse wanted to do something else?) The traditions your family kept helped you define who you were and who your family was.

Give thought to how you want to enjoy holidays, mark milestones, and celebrate rites of passage in your family. Start by basing traditions on your values. Add others you enjoyed from your childhood. If you're married, include those of your spouse as well. Mix in cultural elements if you want. Build some around your children's interests. Give traditions meaning and make them your own.

What traditions do you already have that you enjoy faithfully? What other traditions can you add? Write them down here, and add them to your calendar.

DAY

31

Time is like oxygen—there's a minimum amount that's
necessary for survival. And it takes quantity as well as
quality to develop warm and caring relationships.

ARMAND NICHOLI

For a while, the family buzzwords were "quality time." But the truth is, no substitute exists for quantity of time.

Since busy, single-parent households are so common, and in the majority of two-parent families both parents work, you have to *figure out ways to spend time together.* When my children were teenagers, I gave up golf so that I would have more time available. And Margaret and I always worked especially hard to find time for certain things, such as . . .

- Significant events—birthdays, ball games, recitals, etc.
- Significant needs—never put a family member in crisis on hold.
- Fun times—everybody relaxes and talks more.
- One-on-one time—nothing lets another person know you care more than your undivided attention.

Come up with your own list of ways to spend time with your family.

Write a list of
the ways you are
spending time
with your family.
What creative
ways can you find
to spend more
time together?
What steps can
you take to spend
some significant
time alone with
each other?

DAY

32

*The most important thing a father can do
for his children is love their mother.*
THEODORE HESBURGH

The relational foundation of any family is a couple's marriage. It sets the tone for the household, and it is the model relationship that children learn from more than any other. So *keep your marriage healthy first.* Commitment is what carries you through. If you intend to stay married only as long as you feel the love, don't start. Just like anything else worth fighting for, marriage requires daily discipline and commitment.

It also requires that you *express appreciation for each other.* If people don't receive affirmation and appreciation at home, there's a good chance they won't get it. One of the most positive things you can do for your spouse and children is really get to know them and love them simply because they are yours—not based on performance.

My other suggestion is a reminder to *resolve conflict as quickly as possible.* A family's response to problems will either promote bonding or be destructive. Do it quickly and effectively, and you bring healing. Neglect conflict, and you end with wounds. Develop a strategy for resolving conflict.

What are you doing to keep your marriage healthy? What steps will you take to get to know your spouse and children more and to express your unconditional love for them?

DAY

33

*All that a man achieves or fails to achieve
is the direct result of his thoughts.*
JAMES ALLEN

I was very fortunate to learn about the power of good thinking early in life. My father required me to read for thirty minutes every day. When I was fourteen years old, he had me read *As a Man Thinketh* by James Allen, and today's quote from that book made me realize that my thinking would make or break me. It made such an impression on me that I was prompted to make one of my Daily Dozen decisions: *I will think on things that will add value to myself and others.*

If you desire to make good thinking a daily priority of your life, first you need to *understand that great thinking comes from good thinking.* In order to become a good thinker, you need to be willing to first produce mediocre and downright bad ideas. Only by practicing and developing your thinking daily will your ideas improve. Your thinking ability is determined not by your desire to think, but by your past thinking. To become a good thinker, do more thinking. Once the ideas start flowing, they keep improving.

Describe how you assess your thought life. Have you made good thinking a consistent part of your life? Write a declaration of what you want it to be, sign it, and date it.

....

....

....

....

....

....

....

....

....

....

....

....

....

....

....

....

....

....

....

....

....

DAY

34

Nothing limits achievement like small thinking; nothing expands possibilities like unleashed thinking.

WILLIAM ARTHUR WARD

It's a mistake to believe there is only one kind of thinking. It can cause a person to value only the kind of thinking in which he excels and to dismiss all other types of thinking. I believe eleven different thinking skills come into play when it comes to good thinking. Here is an overview of the first five skills:

1. Big Picture Thinking: the ability to think beyond yourself and your world in order to process ideas with a holistic perspective.

2. Focused Thinking: the ability to think with clarity on issues by removing distractions and mental clutter from your mind.

3. Creative Thinking: the ability to break out of your "box" of limitations and explore ideas and options to experience a breakthrough.

4. Realistic Thinking: the ability to build a solid foundation on facts to think with certainty.

5. Strategic Thinking: the ability to implement plans that give direction for today and increase your potential for tomorrow.

On a scale of 1 to 10 (with 10 being complete mastery), rate your ability for each of the 5 thinking skills. Regarding the skill you rated highest, describe the reasons for why you gave it that rating.

DAY

35

I like to think of thoughts as living blossoms borne by the human tree.
JAMES DOUGLAS

Thinking is multifaceted. It's really a collection of skills. In addition to the five thinking skills I stated yesterday, here are six more good thinking skills.

6. Possibility Thinking: the ability to unleash your enthusiasm and hope to find solutions for even seemingly impossible situations.

7. Reflective Thinking: the ability to revisit the past in order to gain a true perspective and think with understanding.

8. Questioning Popular Thinking: the ability to reject the limitations of common thinking and accomplish uncommon results.

9. Shared Thinking: the ability to include the heads of others to help you think "over your head" and achieve compounding results.

10. Unselfish Thinking: the ability to consider others and their journey to think with collaboration.

11. Bottom-Line Thinking: the ability to focus on results and maximum return to reap the full potential of your thinking.

On a scale of 1 to 10 (with 10 being complete mastery), rate your ability for each of the six thinking skills. Of the 11 thinking skills, which are the two skills you rated highest? Confirm those findings with friends, colleagues, your spouse, or boss.

DAY

36

*No problem can withstand the assault
of sustained thinking.*
VOLTAIRE

Most people are naturally good at a few thinking skills and weak at others. So should you try to master all of them? No, I believe that's a mistake.

Let's say, for example, that you're a very good creative thinker, but you're weak in bottom-line thinking. Rather than devote the tremendous amount of time, energy, and resources to get your bottom-line thinking up to average, give that time to improving your creative thinking instead. Since you are already good, a moderate amount of time and energy could make you excellent. That would enable you to generate ideas and make contributions few others could, giving you a real advantage in your life and career.

So what do you do about your weaknesses? Gather people around you who are strong in those areas. That's what I've done for years, whether it's working as a team with my wife, Margaret, relying on my brother, Larry, or hiring staff who possess strengths in my areas of weakness. Not having to rely entirely on myself when it comes to thinking has been a real advantage for me.

Yesterday you sought out confirmation for the two skills you rated highest of the 11 thinking skills. What steps will you take to focus on these skills? What steps will you take to enlist the help of others in your weakest areas?

DAY

37

For the flower to blossom, you need the right soil as well as the right seed. The same is true to cultivate good thinking.

WILLIAM BERNBACH

When I was in my twenties, I set a priority to practice this discipline of thinking: *Every day I will set aside a time to think, and I will determine to think on the right things.* If you desire to do the same thing, do this:

Find a place to think. Beginning with my first job in 1969, I've always found a place to be my daily thinking spot. Those certainly haven't been the only places I've done my thinking, but they are the ones I've designated for the task. When it comes to what works, everybody's different. Some people like to be connected to nature and others sit alone in a restaurant to think. Where you go doesn't matter as long as it stimulates your thinking.

Set aside think time every day. I do nearly all my best thinking early in the morning—except for reflective thinking, which I usually do in the evenings. I recommend that you try to discover the time of day when your thinking is the sharpest. Then set aside a block of time every day just to think. I believe you'll find that you're much more productive and focused as a result.

If you don't already have a good thinking place and time, you need to find them. Where will you choose to create your thoughts? What is your best thinking time? What block of time will you set aside every day just to think? Write it in your calendar.

DAY

38

For me, when an idea hits me, it strikes fire,
almost like God speaking. I know that sounds heretical,
but there it is. The more time that passes after the idea
strikes, the less heat it gives off. I forget parts of it,
it doesn't seem as great. Ideas have a short half-life.

DAVE GOETZ

To manage the priority of thinking, here are suggestions to add to yesterday's. *Find a process that works for you.* Everybody has a different way of approaching the process of thinking. I don't need anything specific to trigger my thinking. Some people need music or a certain scent. Some think best while at a computer or with a certain pen. Do whatever works for you.

Capture your thoughts. If you don't write down your ideas, there is a great danger you will lose them. When I'm in my thinking spot, I use a legal pad. The rest of the day, I keep a small leather-bound notebook with me. At night, I have something to write with next to my bed. Have a system and use it.

Put your thoughts into action quickly. Have you ever had an idea for a product or service and a few months or years later seen someone else with the same idea take it to market? When you don't do anything with a great idea, you don't reap the results.

What processes and practices have you found in the past that stimulate your thinking? Utilizing them, take a current problem to solve and capture your thoughts by writing them down. Then quickly put your thoughts into action today and write down the results.

DAY

39

*Read not to contradict and confute; nor to believe
and take for granted; nor to find talk and discourse;
but to weigh and consider.*
FRANCIS BACON

My final suggestion to help you manage the priority of thinking is to *try to improve your thinking every day* by doing the following on a daily basis:

Focus on the Positive: Thinking alone won't guarantee success. You need to think about the right things. Negative thinking and worry actually hinder the thinking process rather than improve it. Focus on the positive, and your thinking will move in a positive direction.

Gather Good Input: I've always been a collector of ideas. I do a lot of reading, and I continually file the ideas and quotes I find. The more good ideas I'm exposed to, the more my thinking improves.

Spend Time with Good Thinkers: Well over half of the top executives in any profession had the benefit of being mentored at some time in their careers. And I believe that the greatest benefit anyone receives in that kind of relationship is learning how the mentor thinks. If you spend time with good thinkers, you will find that the exposure sharpens your thinking.

Who are the good thinkers in your life? List them here, and describe how they stretch your thoughts. What steps will you take to cultivate the habit of meeting with these people and benefiting from their insights?

DAY

40

Always bear in mind that your own resolution to success is more important than any other thing.
ABRAHAM LINCOLN

Whatever you think your life purpose or destiny is, to become the person you have the potential to be, you will need great tenacity. That quality comes from commitment that will be tested every day through times of failure, deep disappointment, and when you'll have to stand alone. If you determine to make and keep proper commitments daily, you greatly improve your chances of being able to carry on.

When I was twenty-nine years old, I faced a task that seemed impossible. The success of our church absolutely necessitated a $1 million expansion of our facilities, but as the senior pastor I had never led a major building program. That's when I made one of my Daily Dozen decisions concerning the priority of commitment: *If something is worth doing, I will commit myself to carrying it through.* Little did I realize how much that commitment would be tested with obstacles and problems every day, and how without it, I never would have made it through.

If you desire to have greater tenacity to accomplish the things you desire, make the decision to embrace commitment wholeheartedly in your life.

Where do you stand when it comes to commitment today? What has been your track record? Write a declaration of your priority to embrace commitment wholeheartedly, sign it, and date it.

DAY

41

But if we fail, then the whole world . . . will sink into the abyss of a new dark age. . . . Let us therefore brace ourselves to our duties, and so bear ourselves that, if the British Empire and its Commonwealth last for a thousand years, men will still say, "This was their finest hour."

WINSTON CHURCHILL

In June 1940, with the surrender of France and the British army driven from the European continent, the Germans were certain that Great Britain would seek a peace agreement. But they underestimated the commitment of England's prime minister, Winston Churchill, and of the British people. The war that England fought was long and bloody, and for a long time they suffered terrible bombing and stood alone. But they stood. Their commitment was unwavering. And because they stood, the Allies won the war.

I believe their resolve was strong not only because they knew what was at stake, but they also had a sense of what price they were being asked to pay. It can be very difficult to stand by a commitment naively made. The commitment becomes much stronger when you have already counted the cost. And once you *count the cost*, you have to *decide whether you are really willing to pay the price* and do what it takes to follow through to your prize.

What is the one discipline you must be committed to today and every day in order to succeed? What does it cost? Are you willing to pay the price and follow through to your prize?

DAY

42

*People forget how fast you did a job—
but they remember how well you did it.*
HOWARD W. NEWTON

Few things fire up a person's commitment like *dedication to excellence*. The desire for excellence carried Michelangelo through to the completion of his work on the Sistine Chapel. Excellence drove Edison to keep trying until he figured out how to make a light bulb that worked. Excellence drives the companies Jim Collins wrote about in *Built to Last* and *Good to Great*.

Anyone who desires to achieve and become successful must be like a fine craftsman: committed to excellence. A great craftsman wants you to inspect his work, to look closely at its finest details. In contrast, sloppy people hide their work. And if anyone finds fault with it, shoddy workers find fault with their tools. Which are you most like?

Excellence means doing your very best in everything, in every way. That kind of commitment will take you where half-hearted people will never go.

Consider a job, project, or task you've committed to doing. Describe the standard of excellence you are putting into it—the time, attention, and resources. What can you do to improve that?

DAY

43

The moment one definitely commits oneself, then Providence moves too. All sorts of things occur to help one that would never otherwise have occurred. A whole stream of events issue from the decision, raising in one's favor all manner of unforeseen incidents and meetings and material assistance that no man could have dreamed would come his way.

WILLIAM H. MURRAY

After I made the decision to commit myself to the building program at my church, I knew that I would need to find a way to keep myself on track. So I determined to live out this discipline: *Every day I will renew my commitment and think about the benefits that come from it.* To do that, I carried a laminated card of Murray's quote with me and read it every day for eighteen months. I thought, *If I stay committed and do all I can, and then I ask God to make up the difference, we can achieve this.* And we did!

When you accomplish something that you once believed was impossible, it makes you a new person. It changes the way you see yourself and the world. My thinking went to a new level, and the vision for my leadership expanded. I never would have gotten there without commitment. My personal commitment—and that of many others—was the key to our success.

Describe a task or situation that seems to be impossible for you to accomplish. What will it take to overcome it? Write a statement you can read daily to renew your commitment to making it happen.

DAY

44

The heights by great men reached and kept
Were not attained by sudden flight,
But they, while their companions slept,
Were toiling upward in the night.

HENRY WADSWORTH LONGFELLOW

As you make it a priority to keep your commitments daily, keep the following in mind:

Expect commitment to be a struggle. Anything worth having is going to be a struggle. Commitment doesn't come easy, but when you're fighting for something you believe in, the struggle is worth it. Consider the commitment of the men and women who founded and preserved our country—the risks they took, the battles they fought, the sacrifices they made. The greatest honors were reserved for those who endured the greatest struggles. The stakes were high, but so were the rewards. We still enjoy the freedom they won for us.

Don't rely on talent alone. If you want to reach your potential, you need to add a strong work ethic to your talent. If you want something out of your day, you must put something in it. Your talent is what you were born with. Your skills are what you put in yesterday. Commitment is what you must put in today in order to make today your masterpiece and make tomorrow a success.

94

What is your strategy for winning the battle to stay committed—in your work, important relationships, faith, etc.? What tools will you gather to help you in the fight?

DAY

45

*Nothing is easier than saying words. Nothing is
harder than living them, day after day. What you
promise today must be renewed and redecided tomorrow
and each day that stretches out before you.*
ARTHUR GORDON

In general, people approach the priority of daily commitment in one of two ways. They focus on the external or the internal. Those who focus on the external expect conditions to determine whether they keep their commitments. Because conditions are so transitory, their commitment level changes like the wind. In contrast, people who base their actions on the internal usually focus on their choices. Each choice is a crossroad, one that will either confirm or compromise their commitments. When you come to a crossroad . . .

- A personal decision is required.
- The decision will cost you something.
- Others will likely be influenced by it.

Your choices are the only thing you truly control. You cannot control your circumstances, nor can you control others. *By focusing on your choices, and then making them with integrity, you control your commitment.* And that is what often separates success from failure.

Do you focus on the external or on the internal when it comes to the priority of your daily commitments? What steps will you take today to not allow your circumstances to sway your commitments?

DAY

46

When you're interested in something, you do it only when it's convenient. When you're committed to something, you accept no excuses, only results.
KEN BLANCHARD

Nothing stokes commitment like *single-minded effort* that results in achievement and *doing what's right even when you don't feel like it.* English minister William Carey is a great example of that truth. Although he had only an elementary education, by the time Carey was in his teens, he could read the Bible in six languages. Because of his language skills, he was chosen to be a missionary to India, where he founded the Serampore Mission. A few years after that, he became professor of Oriental languages at Fort William College in Calcutta. He also used his talent with languages in becoming a publisher, printing Bibles in forty languages and dialects for more than three hundred million people.

To what did Carey attribute his success? He said it was because "I can plod. That is my only genius. I can persevere in any definite pursuit. To this I owe everything." If you refuse to give in to excuses, no matter how good they may sound or how good they will make you feel in the moment, you have the potential to go far.

What choices will you make today to take total responsibility for your commitment? How can you become single-minded in your efforts? What truths do you need to embrace to fortify your commitment to do what's right even when you don't feel like it?

DAY

47

The rich rules over the poor,
and the borrower becomes the lender's slave.

SOLOMON

When I was studying for the ministry in 1985, I realized I was choosing a profession where I would not make a lot of money. I didn't mind that because I knew I would be fulfilling what I believed I was called to do. But I also recognized that when a person has no money, he has few options. So Margaret and I made one of our Daily Dozen decisions: *We will sacrifice today so that we can have options tomorrow.* From then on, we've determined to live by this financial formula: 10 percent to church/charity, 10 percent to investments, and 80 percent to living expenses. When our investments have made money, we've rolled the profits over into other investments. Over time our money has been building, and we've enjoyed more options.

The bottom line about money is that it is nothing but a tool. It is good for helping one achieve goals, but the goal of getting money for its own sake is ultimately hollow. Money won't make you happy, but owing money is sure to make you miserable. If you desire to have options, make your finances one of your daily priorities.

Describe where you stand when it comes to finances today. What has been your track record? Write a declaration to make finances one of your daily priorities, sign it, and date it.

....

....

....

....

....

....

....

....

....

....

....

....

....

....

....

....

....

....

....

....

....

....

DAY

48

If a person gets his attitude toward money straight, it will help straighten out almost every other area of his life.
BILLY GRAHAM

If you want to put yourself in a position to make a good decision concerning finances, start by learning to *put the value of things into perspective.* People tend to value money and things over what's really important in life: other people. To know whether your attitude about money and possessions is what it should be, ask yourself these questions:

1. Am I preoccupied with things?

2. Am I envious of others?

3. Do I find my personal value in possessions?

4. Do I believe that money will make me happy?

5. Do I continually want more?

If you answered yes to one or more of these questions, you need to do some soul-searching. Materialism is a mind-set. There's nothing wrong with possessing money or nice things. Likewise, there's nothing wrong with living modestly. Materialism is not about possession—it's an obsession. I've known materialistic people with no money and nonmaterialistic people who possess lots of money. Haven't you?

What is your philosophy concerning money? How did you answer the questions in today's reading? What do you need to change about your relationship to money?

....

....

....

....

....

....

....

....

....

....

....

....

....

....

....

....

....

....

....

DAY

49

Earn all you can, save all you can, give all you can.
JOHN WESLEY

Every phase of life isn't the same, nor should we try to make it that way. Ideally, a person's life should follow a pattern where the main focus goes from learning to earning to returning. When you're young, your focus should be on exploring your talents, discovering your purpose, and learning your trade—and you shouldn't take shortcuts to financial gain and miss the big picture of your life. If you learn your trade well and practice it with excellence, you should be able to earn a good living. And if you work hard and plan well, you may enter a later phase of life that is most rewarding, where you can focus on giving back to others.

These general phases present a pattern for which to strive. If you are young, be patient in the learning phase, because the more diligently you go after phase one, the greater your potential to maximize the other phases. If you're older and you didn't lay a good foundation for yourself, don't despair. Keep learning and growing. You still have a chance to finish well. But if you give up, you'll never go up.

What must you do to maximize the phase of life you are in today? Looking ahead to the next phase, what can you do better now to prepare for the future?

DAY

50

*Every person in debt is suffering from some type of
depression. Debt is one of the leading causes of divorce,
lack of sleep, and poor work performance. It is truly one of
the deep dark secrets that people have. It robs them of their
self-worth and keeps them from achieving dreams.*
MICHAEL KIDWELL AND STEVE RHODE

I have two more suggestions to help you make a good
decision concerning the priority of finances. One is to
reduce your debt. Going into debt for things that appreciate
in value can be a good idea. Purchasing a house, securing
transportation so you can work, improving your education, and investing in a business are good things—as long
as you manage them well. But many people incur debt for
frivolous things. When you're still paying for something
you no longer use or even have, it means trouble. Don't
let your possessions or your lifestyle possess you. If you're
a slave to debt, find a way to free yourself.

The other suggestion is to *put your financial formula
into place.* If you haven't decided to plan your finances,
you're headed for trouble. Put yourself on a budget.
Create a financial formula that works for you. You may
want to try the 10-10-80 approach that Margaret and I
use. But do something! The old saying is corny but true:
Failing to plan is like planning to fail.

What do you owe money on? What concerns do you have? What sort of financial formula do you have in place to handle the day-to-day management of your money? If you don't have one, figure out one that works for you, write a declaration to follow it, sign it, and date it.

DAY

51

Money is a terrible master but an excellent servant.
P. T. BARNUM

Finances were once so low on my list of priorities that for a time I neglected them, but I discovered that I had no right to neglect finances just because it wasn't an area of strength or passion for me. So now, at home and in business, I maintain this discipline: *Every day I will focus on my financial game plan so that each day I will have more, not fewer, options.* The earlier you make the decision and practice the discipline of sound financial management, the more options you will have.

I believe the first discipline of finances is to *maximize your earning potential.* By that I don't mean to neglect the other important areas of life in order to make a buck. Nor am I suggesting that your focus should always be on money. Just maintain a strong work ethic, and learn how to make and manage money. Develop relationships with people who are successful in this area and learn from them. Read good books about personal and business finances. With the right attitude and a willingness to pay the price, almost anyone can pursue nearly any opportunity and achieve it.

What are you doing every day to maximize your earning potential? How do you describe your work ethic and knowledge of managing your money? What steps will you take today to improve that?

DAY

52

Americans have always been stricken by the disease that some have called "luxury fever" or "affluenza." Even if we aren't rich yet, we'd like to look as if we were.

JAMES SUROWIECKI

One of the most important things you can do for yourself is keep your perspective and *be grateful every day* for whatever you have. If you work hard and maintain an attitude of gratitude, you'll find it easier to manage your finances every day.

Another important thing is to *not compare yourself to others.* Whenever people start comparing themselves to others, they get into trouble. Comparisons of money and possessions can be especially detrimental. Wanting to keep up with neighbors or appear well-off gets many people into horrible debt.

If you see your neighbors buying new home furnishings, taking elaborate vacations, and driving a new vehicle every year, does something stir inside you to do the same? Just because someone appears to be in similar circumstances to you doesn't mean anything. Your neighbors might earn twice as much as you do. Or they may be in debt up to their eyeballs. Don't make assumptions, and don't try to be like someone else.

Write an honest assessment of your daily gratitude level and the degree to which "affluenza" and comparing yourself to others afflicts you. What do you need to do to increase your gratitude and decrease the comparisons?

DAY

53

Money is like manure. If you let it pile up,
it just smells. But if you spread it around,
you can encourage things to grow.
GUN DENHART

One other financial discipline is practicing the priority of *giving as much as you can.* Author Bruce Larson says, "Money is another pair of hands to heal and feed and bless the desperate families of the earth.... In other words, money is my other self. Money can go where I do not have time to go, where I do not have a passport to go. My money can go in my place and heal and bless and feed and help. A man's money is an extension of himself." That's true of your money only if you're willing to part with it.

Blaise Pascal said, "I love poverty because Jesus loved it. I love wealth because it affords me the means of helping the needy. I keep faith with everyone." The past few days I've mentioned financial "options," which for me is about service. Philanthropist Andrew Carnegie said his goal was to spend the first half of his life accumulating wealth and the second half giving it away. What a great idea! My desire is to spend my future years giving to others, and what matters is that I do what I can.

What compounding benefits do you expect to receive from your priority toward your finances? What cause that is close to your heart might you be able to help financially if you were to improve your financial situation?

DAY

54

Faith keeps the person who keeps the faith.
MOTHER TERESA

Some people have ambivalent feelings about my opinions regarding faith. And some may be offended. If that is true for you, please feel free to simply skip the next six readings. However, knowing my background, you're probably not surprised that faith is one of my Daily Dozen life priorities, because I sincerely believe that faith holds the key to life's meaning.

I grew up in a household filled with faith. But you can't live on someone else's faith. There are no spiritual grandchildren. Each person must make his or her own decision and act on it with integrity. At age seventeen, I made my faith decision: *I will accept God's gift of his Son, Jesus Christ, as my Savior.* That decision, more than any other, has shaped my life and forged my worldview. Recognition of God's love for everyone has influenced how I view others. The Golden Rule has taught me how to treat people. God's love for me has given me great self-worth. And the Bible has taught me everything I know about leadership. Therefore, I hope to encourage you to explore making faith one of your personal priorities.

Where do you stand when it comes to faith today? What or who have you placed your faith in? Are you confident in your faith decision?

DAY

55

*Faith is at the heart of life. You go to a doctor
whose name you cannot pronounce. He gives you a
prescription you cannot read. You take it to a pharmacist
you have never seen. He gives you a medicine you
do not understand and yet you take it.*

JOHN BISAGNO

The underlying message from God is not to act differently, but to become different. Not to act honestly, but to become an honest person. Then honesty will be at the core of your life. My faith has not only given me peace; it has given me a wonderful model for life.

If you desire to make an honest exploration of faith, know this: *We all have faith . . . the important choice is where we place it.* Every day we act on beliefs that have little or no evidence to back them up. That is also true in a spiritual sense. Just as one person has faith that God is real, an atheist has faith that there is no God. Both people hold strong beliefs, and neither person can produce evidence to absolutely prove his point of view. Right now, you already have faith in something. Your goal should be to align your beliefs with the truth. Seek the truth, and I believe you will find it.

In what ways have you made an honest exploration of faith? What steps will you take to seek the truth and to align your beliefs to the truth?

DAY

56

*The steps of faith fall on the seeming void
and find the rock beneath.*
WALT WHITMAN

Some people see faith as a sign of weakness. If faith is new to you and you are uncertain how to approach it, I would advise you to view it as an opportunity for a course correction in the journey of life. In a play by T. S. Eliot, one character expresses it in those kinds of terms. He describes a *faith that comes after extreme disappointment.* He calls it the "kind of faith that arises after despair. The destination cannot be described; you will know very little until you get there; you will journey blind. But the way leads toward possession of what you have sought for in the wrong place."

If you are experiencing difficulties, allow yourself to explore faith in response to it. Henri Nouwen said this "is the great conversation in our life: to recognize and believe that many unexpected events are not just disturbing interruptions of our projects, but the way in which God molds our hearts and prepares us." Faith not only can help you through a crisis, it can help you to approach life after the hard times with a whole new outlook of hope and courage through faith to face reality.

Do you consider yourself a person of faith? In what ways does your faith or spirituality help in difficult times? If you are not a person of faith, are you willing to explore the possibility of God? What steps might you take in that direction?

DAY

57

*The sweetest thing in all my life has been the longing . . .
to find the place where all the beauty came from.*

C. S. LEWIS

Exploring and deepening your faith is very similar to getting yourself into good physical condition through regular exercise. Perhaps that's why the Bible contains so many athletic metaphors for spiritual growth. One way to explore your faith is to *associate with people of faith.* It's a fact that you become more like the people you spend time with. If you desire to increase your faith, spend time with others who exercise theirs. Learn from them. Find out how they think.

I also recommend that you follow the advice of how D. L. Moody, a nineteenth-century lay preacher who founded Northfield Seminary and the Moody Bible Institute, developed his faith. He said, "I prayed for faith, and thought that some day faith would come down and strike me like lightning. But faith did not seem to come. One day I read in the tenth chapter of Romans, 'Faith comes by hearing, and hearing by the word of God.' I had closed my Bible and prayed for faith. I now opened my Bible and began to study, and faith has been growing ever since."

List the people you know whom you respect concerning their faith. Set up a time to meet with them. Also write down the questions you have about faith, about any books they might recommend, and about a community of believers with whom they recommend that you connect.

DAY

58

Faith draws the poison from every grief,
takes the sting from every loss, and quenches the
fire of every pain; and only faith can do it.
S. G. HOLLAND

It's not enough to simply make a faith decision. If you want to live it out, you have to work at deepening it. Faith gives you peace and strength only if it's not superficial. The deeper the faith, the greater its potential to carry you through the rough times. *A faith that hasn't been tested can't be trusted.* As Rabbi Abraham Heschel said, "Faith like Job's cannot be shaken because it is the result of having been shaken."

Perhaps nothing in recent history tested the faith of so many people as severely as the Holocaust. Viennese psychiatrist Victor Frankl was one of the survivors of the Nazi atrocities. He spent 1942 to 1945 in the concentration camps of Auschwitz and Dachau. Frankl once said, "A weak faith is weakened by predicaments and catastrophes whereas a strong faith is strengthened by them." Despite the horrors he witnessed and the treatment he suffered, his faith didn't weaken—it deepened. When you believe in something, you have something to live for. And that keeps you going, even under extremely difficult circumstances.

Has your faith undergone a period of testing? How so? Did it stand the test and grow deeper, or did you let it fall to the wayside? What steps can you take today to deepen your faith?

DAY

59

*Faith is trusting in advance what
will only make sense in reverse.*
PHILLIP YANCEY

To help you manage your priority of faith, *embrace
the value of faith.* There is a spiritual aspect to human life
that cannot be denied. Spiritual needs must be met spiri-
tually. Nothing else will fill the void. There are longings
of the soul that can be satisfied only with spiritual experiences, though people try and fail to meet them in material ways. Faith allows the soul to go beyond what the
eyes can see. Not only does faith give a person strength,
it also makes them more resilient. I cannot imagine how
my life would have played out without my faith at the
center of it.

For me, managing the discipline of faith can be cap-
tured in one simple phrase: *Every day to live and lead like
Jesus.* While the words are simple, following through is
not. Living out the priority of faith is the greatest challenge of my Daily Dozen. The problem is that instead of
being like Jesus, I often want to be like John Maxwell. I
fall short of the mark. But with God as my helper, I keep
growing. And when I do follow in his footsteps and live
his principles, people are helped and I am fulfilled.

Does your faith satisfy the spiritual needs of your soul? Describe what your soul desires and how your faith fulfills that. What compounding benefits do you expect to receive through making your faith a daily priority?

DAY

60

*Unbelief puts our circumstances between us and God. Faith
puts God between us and our circumstances. Who wouldn't
like to have the Creator of the universe helping them? James,
one of the fathers of the first-century church, advised,
"Come near to God and he will come near to you."*

F. B. MEYER

To help you make a priority of the discipline of faith,
put God in the picture. Many people hope that science
will provide all the answers to life's questions. But science
cannot do that. Ironically, what is embraced as scientific
fact often changes. Contrast science with faith. The core
beliefs of Judaism and Christianity, which address our
spiritual needs, have not changed in thousands of years.

There's a story of a man driving a convertible on a
mountain road that missed a sharp turn and went right
over the edge. As his car plunged to the canyon floor, he
managed to grab on to a tree sprouting from the cliff face.
"Help!" he screamed. "Can anyone hear me?" Silence.
"God, can you hear me?" Suddenly a voice thundered,
"Yes, I can." "Will you help me?" "Yes. Do you believe in
me?" "Yes!" "Do you trust me?" "Yes, yes! Please, hurry!"
"If you trust me, let go of the tree." After a long silence,
the man cried, "Can anyone else hear me?" Having faith is
about putting your trust in what you cannot see.

How are you presently putting your faith in the picture of your life? What steps will you take to understand and make the core beliefs of your faith a daily part of your life?

DAY

*Relationships help us to define who we
are and what we can become. Most of us can
trace our successes to pivotal relationships.*
DONALD O. CLIFTON AND PAULA NELSON

All the significant accomplishments in the history
of humankind have been achieved by teams of people.
That truth can also be carried over to a personal level.
Most of life's great moments—the ones that resonate in
our hearts and minds—involve other people. When you
understand that being connected to others is one of life's
greatest joys, you realize that life's best comes when you
initiate and invest in solid relationships.

As a young person, I developed good people skills,
but when I heard my college psychology professor, Dr.
David Van Hoose, state, "If you have one true friend in
life, you are very fortunate. If you have two real friends, it
is highly unusual," I was dumbfounded. I determined to
be more intentional and take relationships to a new level
in my life. That's when I made the priority of relationships one of my Daily Dozen decisions: *I will initiate and
make an investment in relationships with others.*

To have the kind of solid relationships that bring fulfillment, you have to take responsibility and be intentional
in making it one of your most significant priorities.

Where do you stand when it comes to the priority of relationships today? What has been your history? Write a declaration to make relationships one of your daily priorities, sign it, and date it.

....

....

....

....

....

....

....

....

....

....

....

....

....

....

....

....

....

DAY

*You can make more friends in two months by becoming
interested in other people than you can in two years by
trying to get other people interested in you.*

DALE CARNEGIE

We tend to revere rugged individualists, but there are
no real-life Rambos or Lone Rangers who do things of
great achievement on their own. Consultant John Luther
observes, "Natural talent, intelligence, a wonderful education—none of these guarantees success. Something else is
needed: the sensitivity to understand what other people
want and the willingness to give it to them. Worldly success depends on pleasing others."

There's an old saying in sales: All things being equal,
the likable person wins. But all things not being equal, the
likable person still wins. *There's no substitute for relational
skill when it comes to getting ahead in any aspect of life.*
People who alienate others have a hard time. Here's why:

- People who don't like you will try to hurt you.
- If they can't hurt you . . . they won't help you.
- If they have to help you . . . they won't hope you
  succeed.
- When they hope you don't succeed . . . life's vic-
  tories feel hollow.

What do you think other people would say about your relational skills? What can you begin to do today to improve them?

DAY

63

You can't make the other fellow feel important in your presence if you secretly feel that he is a nobody.
LES GIBLIN

Let's face it, if you don't care about people, you are unlikely to make building good relationships a priority in your life. You first need to *place a high value on people*. Expect the best from everyone. Assume people's motives are good unless they prove them to be otherwise. Value them by their best moments. And give them your friendship rather than asking for theirs. That will ultimately be their decision.

Next, you need to *improve your understanding of people* so that you can build positive relationships. Keep in mind the following truths about people: People are insecure . . . give them confidence. People want to feel special . . . sincerely compliment them. People desire a better tomorrow . . . show them hope. People need to be understood . . . listen to and encourage them. People are selfish . . . speak to their needs first. People want to be associated with success . . . help them win.

When you understand people, don't take their shortcomings personally, and help them to succeed, you lay the groundwork for good relationships.

What is your natural bent when it comes to dealing with people? What discipline must you practice today and every day to place a higher value on people?

DAY

64

*Always start a relationship by asking: Do I have ulterior
motives for wanting to relate to this person? Is my caring
conditional? Am I planning to change the person? Do I
need this person to help me make up for a deficiency in
myself? If your answer to any of these questions is yes, leave
the person alone. He or she is better off without you.*

LEO BUSCAGLIA

To have the kind of solid relationships that bring fulfillment, *give respect freely but expect to earn it from others.*
Every human being deserves to be treated with respect
because everyone has value. I have observed that giving
people respect first is one of the most effective ways of
interacting with others. However, that doesn't mean you
can demand respect in return. You must earn it. If you
respect yourself, respect others, and exhibit competence,
others will almost always give you respect.

Another key to building great relationships is to
commit yourself to adding value to others. You do that by
looking for ability in others, helping others discover their
ability, and helping others develop their ability. Some
people are willing to add value, but only if they expect to
receive value in return. If you want to make relationships
a priority, you must check your motives to be sure you are
not trying to manipulate others for your own gain.

Write down the name of someone with whom you really struggle to have a good relationship. What does it mean to give that person respect but expect to earn it from him or her? What will you do today to add value to that person?

DAY

65

Do unto others as you would have them do unto you.
THE GOLDEN RULE

Good relationships require a lot of effort. To keep me on track in my relationships so that I'm investing in them as I must to make them successful, I practice this discipline: *Every day I make the conscious effort to deposit goodwill into my relationships with others.* That means I give more than I expect to receive, love others unconditionally, look for ways to add value to others, and bring joy to the relationships I hold dear. Every evening, I evaluate this area of my life by asking myself, "Have I been thoughtful toward people today? Would they express joy that they have spent time with me?" If the answer is yes, I've done my part.

If you want to improve your relationships through your everyday actions, the most basic way to do that is to *put others first* by practicing the Golden Rule. If you take that mind-set into all your interactions with others, you can't go wrong. But there are also other ways to show people they matter and that you are interested in their well-being: Remember people's names, smile at everyone, and be quick to offer help.

Write down the names of three people to whom you will bring words of encouragement today. Once you have accomplished that, return here and write down the positive impact that had upon them as well as you.

DAY

66

When you hold resentment toward another,
you are bound to that person or condition by an
emotional link that is stronger than steel. Forgiveness
is the only way to dissolve that link and get free.

CATHERINE PONDER

Few things weigh down relationships as much as old hurts and offenses carried day after day in a person's life. If you want to enjoy your time with other people, you've got to *get rid of emotional baggage.* You can't keep score of old wrongs and expect to make relationships right. If someone has hurt you, address it and get it out onto the table right away. Resolve it and get beyond it. If it's not worth bringing up, forget about it and move on.

If you're like most people, you give away your relational energy and time on a first-come, first-served basis. That's why the squeaky wheels instead of the high producers at work consume so much attention and why so many people have nothing left to give when they get home from work. Make it your priority to *give your relational energy and time to your most valuable relationships.* I believe your family should come first as you plan to spend your time. After that should come your next most important relationships. It's a matter of practicing good priorities.

Describe a relationship in which you are carrying emotional baggage. Write out a plan of action for how you will deal with it and date it when you have accomplished it.

DAY

67

*Life is an exciting business and
most exciting when lived for others.*
HELEN KELLER

The longer I live, the more convinced I am that adding value to others is the greatest thing we can do in this life. Because of that, *when I serve, I try to do so cheerfully and with the greatest impact.* That came into special focus after I had my heart attack. More than anything else in those moments of pain when I wasn't sure whether I would live or die, I wanted to tell the people closest to me how much I loved them. I learned that *you can't tell the people you love how much you love them too often.*

Many people believe the best way they can help others is to criticize them, to give them the benefit of their "wisdom." I disagree. The best way to help people is to *see the best in them and encourage them.* I want them to know the good I see in them. I practice the 101 percent principle. I look for the 1 thing I admire in them and give them 100 percent encouragement for it. It helps me to like them. It helps them to like me. And what else could be better for starting a relationship?

Pick a person to whom you want to express your love today. Write down the abilities that you see in them, the ways that you will help them discover their abilities, and the commitment you are making to help them develop their abilities. Then follow through and tell them.

DAY

68

The world of the generous gets larger and larger; the world of the stingy gets smaller and smaller. The one who blesses others is abundantly blessed; those who help others are helped.

SOLOMON

When my wife, Margaret, and I started our life together in the weeks after our wedding, we moved to Hillham, Indiana, where I took my first job. The church that hired me was able to pay only $80 a week, so Margaret worked several jobs to help us make ends meet. Those were difficult days for us financially, yet they were still filled with great joy.

At that time, my brother, Larry, and his wife, Anita, saw that we were struggling, and they were very generous to us. Their generous spirit was such a tremendous source of joy for them and a blessing for us, and I realized the incredible value of having a generous lifestyle. That's when I made another of my Daily Dozen life decisions: *I will live to give.*

Margaret and I recognized that greatness is defined by what a person gives. True generosity isn't a function of income—it begins with the heart. It's about serving others and looking for ways to add value to them. If you make a priority of generosity, you will achieve significance in your life.

Where do you stand when it comes to generosity? Honestly review your financial records and assess your history of giving. Write a declaration to make generosity one of your daily priorities, sign it, and date it.

DAY

No man can live happily who regards himself alone,
who turns everything to his own advantage. You must
live for others if you wish to live for yourself.

SENECA

Perhaps you need some convincing regarding making the priority of generosity. There are many reasons, but here are just three:

First, no one likes to be around people who think only of themselves. In contrast, nearly everyone enjoys being around people who are giving. This is true because *giving turns your focus outward*—from self to others. When you're occupied with helping others succeed, it drives away selfishness. And that not only makes the world a better place, it makes the giver happier.

Second, *giving adds value to others*, which is one of the most significant things a person can do while on this earth. In this life, the measure of a person isn't the number of people who serve him or the amount of money he amasses; it's how many people he serves. The greater your giving, the greater you're living.

Third, *giving helps the giver*. When you help others, you can't help but benefit. You can't light another's path without casting light on your own.

Since giving starts with the heart, what is the one discipline regarding generosity you must practice today and every day in order to be successful?

....

....

....

....

....

....

....

....

....

....

....

....

....

....

....

....

....

....

....

....

DAY

70

Where your treasure is, there your heart will be also.

JESUS

The way people handle money colors their attitude about many other aspects of their lives. Wherever your money is, that's where your attention goes. Haven't you found that to be true? If you invest in the stock market, you probably check the financial page or your earning statements frequently. If you spend a large amount of money on a house, you probably spend a lot of time and effort taking care of it.

If you desire to become generous and make generosity part of your daily life, *give others your money*. If you give money to people, either directly or through a worthy charity, you will care about people more. And that will help to foster a more generous spirit in you. You have to "prime the pump" so to speak, and then the giving will flow. If you wait until you feel like giving, you may wait forever. You become generous by first giving money away. Andrew Carnegie, the steel magnate who gave away millions of dollars, said, "No man becomes rich unless he enriches others."

Write down the name of a person or charity in real financial need. Set an amount of money to give and write out how you will follow through on getting that money to them, either anonymously or in person. Record how you felt.

DAY

71

The purpose of life is not to win. The purpose of life is to grow and to share. When you come to look back on all that you have done in life, you will get more satisfaction from the pleasure you brought to other people's lives than you will from the times that you outdid and defeated them.

HAROLD KUSHNER

What do people often value more than your money? The answer is your time and attention. Take a moment to recall the people who've had the greatest impact in your life. Maybe you had a parent, aunt, or uncle who made you feel loved and accepted. Or perhaps a teacher or coach or employer saw your potential, painted a positive picture of your future, and then challenged and helped you to become the person you were always meant to be. What gift could be greater than that?

If you desire to become generous and make generosity part of your daily life, *give others yourself.* The people closest to you would rather have you than your money. Even perceptive employees with great potential understand that a good mentor is more valuable than a mere monetary reward. When you invest in another person just for the sake of seeing them blossom, you will be the kind of generous person others want to be around. And your days truly will be masterpieces.

What do you have to invest in another person? What skills do you possess that someone would benefit from learning? What life experiences have you had that can help another person? What resources do you possess that ought to be shared? Write out your list.

DAY

72

You are not here merely to make a living. You are here in order to enable the world to live more amply, with greater vision, with a finer spirit of home and achievement. You are here to enrich the world, and you impoverish yourself if you forget the errand.

WOODROW WILSON

It's very easy to live only for yourself. But we can take another path—to be generous. My desire is to be the kind of person I would like to be around. To help with that, I practice the priority of this discipline, reminding myself: *Every day I will add value to others.*

What does it mean to add value to others? How do you do it? Here is how to start:

- *Value People:* This means treating everyone with respect.
- *Know What People Value:* This means listening and seeking to understand others.
- *Make Yourself More Valuable:* This means growing in order to give, because you cannot give what you do not possess.

When you value people, you open the door to generosity. And it becomes much easier to plan for and model generosity daily.

Set an unselfish goal for yourself to add value to three people today. Write down their names and the specific actions or words you will give them. After you have followed through, write down their reactions.

DAY

73

Watch lest prosperity destroy generosity.
HENRY WARD BEECHER

As you strive to practice the discipline of generosity every day, *don't wait for prosperity to become generous.* I've heard many people say that if they ever get a lot of money, they will become generous. People who say such things are usually fooling themselves.

A person's level of income and their desire to give have nothing to do with one another. Prosperity and high income don't help people become generous. Some of the most generous people I know have nothing materially. And I know plenty of people who have a lot to give but no heart to give it. Statistics bear that out.

People give not from the top of their purses, but from the bottom of their hearts. If you desire to become a more generous person, don't wait for your income to change. Change your heart. Do that, and you can become a giver regardless of your income or circumstances.

What holds you back from being generous with your time and money when you see people or organizations in need? What steps will you take today to break through those walls and let your heart do what it really wants to do?

....

....

....

....

....

....

....

....

....

....

....

....

....

....

....

....

....

....

....

....

DAY

74

*[I am] privileged to be the heir to huge wealth
and I regard myself as custodian of that money for
the benefit of people who need it more than I do.*
J. PAUL GETTY JR.

It may be easy for people to find reasons not to give. But it's just as easy to find good reasons to give. You just need to look for them. J. Paul Getty was recognized by *Fortune* magazine in 1957 as the richest man in the world, and yet he seemed to have many reasons not to give. His stinginess became as legendary as his wealth. Yet one of his sons, J. Paul Getty Jr., was his opposite. He gave millions of dollars of his fortune away, which was only a fraction of the Getty fortune. Become like the younger Getty.

Go out of your way to *find reasons to give every day*. Look for a compelling cause. Find an urgent need. Look for a group that is making an impact. Seek out leaders you know and believe in. Give to organizations you respect and trust. They're all around you; you just need to make it a priority.

Remember: What we do for ourselves alone dies with us, but what we do for others and the world remains and is immortal.

Turn on the intuitive radar of your heart to look for human needs today. What needs do you perceive and feel prompted to help? Write out how you will follow through on that inclination.

DAY

75

*Do all the good you can, to all the people you can,
in all the ways you can, as long as you can.*
D. L. MOODY

When it comes right down to it, the recipients of your generosity are never causes, institutions, or organizations. Ultimately, the recipients are individual people.

People in need of help are all around you. You don't need to go halfway around the world or send a check overseas to help and serve others, although there's nothing wrong with doing those things. But there are plenty of people closer to home who can benefit from what you have to offer—people in your own town, your own neighborhood, even your own home. *Being generous means keeping your eyes open for opportunities to give to everyone,* whether it's through mentoring a colleague, feeding a homeless person, sharing your faith with a friend, or spending time with your kids. Civil rights leader Martin Luther King Jr. said, "Life's most persistent and urgent question is, 'What are we doing for others?'" How you answer that question is a measure of your generosity. And the more generous you are, the greater your opportunity to do something significant for others.

List the three people closest to you and write down what each person values, what's important to them. Then brainstorm ideas for how you can add value to them and the specific ways you will do that.

DAY

76

Back of every life there are principles that have fashioned it.
GEORGE H. LORIMER

What admirable character qualities do you want to possess? Think over the various aspects of your life—attitude, health, family, faith, relationships, profession, etc.—and try to determine what is important to you about each. This is where your values come from.

When I was twenty-three years old, I read *Spiritual Leadership* by J. Oswald Sanders. It changed my life. Although I grew up in a home where great values were taught and lived out, until then I had been a people pleaser in my leadership. Ninety percent of the time that was okay. But on the occasions when a leadership decision was required to do something that would be unpopular, I wavered. I realized that I hadn't been leading according to my values, and this realization gave me the courage to do the right thing, even if it wasn't popular. I made the Daily Dozen life decision: *I will lead others based on the values I embrace.*

If you want your life to exhibit the qualities you find desirable and to live with integrity, you need to know what your values are, embrace them, and practice them every day.

Where do you stand when it comes to living your life according to your values? Assess your track record from the past. Write a declaration to make values one of your daily priorities, sign it, and date it.

DAY

77

When I lay down the reins of this administration, I want to have one friend left, and that friend is inside myself.
ABRAHAM LINCOLN

Your core values are the deeply held beliefs that authentically describe your soul and become a companion to you throughout your life. That can be very reassuring, as noted by President Lincoln.

Why do values matter? Because *strong core values are the principles that guide and anchor you on the ocean of life.* When life's waves come crashing down, you will not be put under. Strong currents are not liable to take you places you don't want to go.

Just like your circumstances, the way you live your life is constantly changing. You acquire new skills, disciplines, and habits. Practices always change according to the situation, but values don't. They are always dependable to guide you. Methods are many, values are few.

Once you have thoroughly examined your values and articulated them, you will be able to steer your life by them. You may add to your list as you become older and wiser, but if something is truly a core value, it remains one for life.

Write down your philosophy about core values. Describe a core value that you hold onto in contrast to the changing methods you use as situations change.

....

....

....

....

....

....

....

....

....

....

....

....

....

....

....

....

....

....

....

DAY

78

*Authentic values are those by which a
life can be lived, which can form a people that
produces great deeds and thoughts.*
ALLAN BLOOM

If you know your values and live by them every day, you will have few regrets at the end of your life. To help you get started, *create a list of good values.* Begin writing down every admirable character quality you can think of concerning values, and try to capture what's important to you about it. Ultimately, your values should not be determined by externals, such as your profession or your environment.

When you think you've exhausted every possible idea, set the list aside for a while but keep thinking about it in the back of your mind. When new ideas come, add them to the list. You may want to do some reading to expand your thinking. After a few weeks, combine common ideas on the list and narrow it down. You can't possibly live out twenty, so you need to eliminate anything that's superficial or temporary. Which are based on truth and your highest ideals? Which items truly represent the core of your being? Which will be lasting? What would you be willing to live for? To die for?

Create a list of good values as described in this reading and write them down, then select the values you desire to live out.

DAY

79

Try not to become men of success.
Rather, become men of value.
ALBERT EINSTEIN

Years ago my friend Jim Dobson, the founder of Focus on the Family, spoke about the issue of a midlife crisis. He said, "I believe that it is more a phenomenon of a wrong value system than it is the age group in which it occurs. All of a sudden you realize that the ladder you've been climbing is leaning against the wrong wall." *Clarifying and embracing your values* can help you to prevent such an occurrence from happening to you.

True life change begins when you decide to change your value system, because it's foundational to everything you do. My friend Pat Williams, senior vice president of the Orlando Magic, once told me that when Roy Disney was asked about the secret of Disney's success, he used to say that the company was managed by values, which led to ease in good decision making. The same is true for an individual. Having values keeps a person focused on the important things. That leads to a better quality of life, a life of integrity. Besides, if you focus on your values, success is likely to follow anyway.

Spend some time in reflection on your list of core values from yesterday. What values have you been embracing and not embracing? What will you do today to improve your integrity and focus upon living by your core values?

DAY

80

Don't compromise yourself. You are all you've got.
JANIS JOPLIN

Managing your life according to your values isn't easy. Why? Because your values will be tested daily by those who do not embrace them. Negative people may discount you when you display a positive attitude. People may not understand your devotion to your family or your dedication to personal growth. And those whose priorities are different from yours will try to convince you to follow them or make unwise compromises.

The discipline I practice to battle this is simple: *Every day I review and reflect on my values.* To help me do that, I keep a list of my Daily Dozen in my "thinking companion," a little notebook I always keep with me so that I can write down ideas and jot down reminders of things to tell Margaret. Every time I open the notebook, I see those twelve values. I also give myself the twelve-minute test. At the end of each day, I spend one minute reviewing and reflecting on each of the Daily Dozen. That way, I stay on track and am less likely to drift away from living out my values.

At the end of the day, review and write down how your practices compared to your values. Set aside time and designate a place to reflect every day on your values and write it in your calendar.

DAY

81

All of us are experts at practicing virtue at a distance.
THEODORE HESBURGH

To become better at practicing your values every day, *articulate and embrace your values daily.* After you've created your list of values, write a descriptive statement for each one explaining how you intend to apply it to your life and what benefit or direction that will bring. Keep that document where you can see and think about your values every day. As you go through your day and face decisions, measure your choices against your values. And whenever it's appropriate, talk about them. It not only cements your values in your mind and helps you to practice them, but it also adds a level of accountability.

Then you need to *compare your values to your practices daily.* The gap between knowing and doing is significantly greater than the gap between ignorance and knowledge. A person who identifies and articulates his or her values but doesn't practice them is like a salesperson who fails to deliver on a promise. Even if you are unaware of your behavior and are not doing it intentionally, it demonstrates a lack of credibility. In business, that leads to losing a job. In life, that leads to losing integrity and a life of chaos.

Utilizing the list of core values you made on day 78, write a descriptive statement for each one as described in this reading. Use this list as a means to help you compare your values to your practices as you spend time in reflection at the end of every day.

DAY

82

Nice guys may appear to finish last,
but usually they are running in a different race.
KEN BLANCHARD
AND NORMAN VINCENT PEALE

Many people get into trouble when their values and their feelings collide. When you're feeling good and everything's going your way, it's not difficult to consistently live out your values. However, when your values determine you should take an action that will hurt or cost you something, it can be harder to follow through. For instance, if you saw your boss stealing from the company and you knew that calling attention to it would get you fired and/or ruin you financially.

Successful people *do what's right no matter how they feel about it.* They don't expect to be able to feel their way into acting. They act first and then hope that their feelings follow suit. Usually that doesn't involve anything dramatic. The tough decisions are the everyday ones. For example, if good health is one of my values, will I exercise even though I don't feel like it? Will I refrain from eating a big piece of chocolate cake even though I really want it? To be successful, my values—not my feelings—need to control my actions.

Describe a situation where you did what's right despite how you felt, then describe a situation where you didn't do what you knew was right because of how you felt. What truths can you tell yourself in the future to fortify always taking a stand for what's right?

DAY

83

No man, for any considerable period, can wear one face to himself and another to the multitude, without finally getting bewildered as to which may be the true.

NATHANIEL HAWTHORNE

Most people take very little time to do any reflective thinking, yet that is necessary for anyone who wants to live out his values with consistency. Ben Franklin used to get up in the morning asking himself, "What good will I do today?" When he went to bed, he asked himself, "What good did I do today?" He was evaluating himself in light of one of his values. I've tried to do something similar. At the end of the day, I reflect on whether I've added value to anyone's life during the day, because that is something I desire to do every day. My values have provided a solid foundation on which I have built my life. At times, my value-based leadership has alienated me from others, but never from myself.

By choosing to embrace and practice good values every day, you *choose the higher course in life.* And your life goes in a direction that you will always feel good about. You may not always get what you desire, but you will always be the person you desire to be.

In the morning, write down the good you are going to do today. And before you go to bed, write down the good you have done. Did you do so according to your values and integrity? Make this a habit every day to keep yourself on track.

DAY

84

*To be what we are, and to become what we are
capable of becoming, is the only end of life.*
ROBERT LOUIS STEVENSON

In 1974, I met with Kurt Campmeier of Success Motivation, Inc., who asked me, "John, what is your plan for personal growth?" After having talked for ten minutes about how hard I worked and the gains I was making in my organization, I ran out of things that might qualify as growth. And that's when it hit me. I wasn't doing anything intentional or strategic to make myself better. Up till then I had always believed in my own potential, but I had never thought about having a way to increase and reach it. And in that moment, I made the Daily Dozen decision: *I will develop and follow a personal growth plan for my life.*

Nearly all people would like to become who they are capable of being, yet many people don't. One reason is that they think growth is automatic as you age, that it comes from information or as you have experiences. These may aid in your growth, but if you don't make personal growth a life priority through a commitment to continuous improvement to reach your potential, it won't happen.

What is your plan for personal growth? Be honest in your assessment. Write a declaration to make personal growth one of your daily priorities, sign it, and date it.

DAY

85

*The only thrill worthwhile is the one that comes
from making something out of yourself.*
WILLIAM FEATHER

If you're ready to make the decision to pursue growth and experience improvement every day, begin by answering the question: *What is your potential?* What dreams do you have that are just waiting to be fulfilled? What gifts and talents are inside you that are dying to be drawn out and developed? The gap between your vision and your present reality can only be filled through a commitment to maximize your potential.

To make something out of yourself, you need to *be willing to change*, for without change, there can be no growth. The problem most people have is that they want things to stay the same yet also get better. Obviously, that can't happen. If you truly want to grow, commit yourself to not only accepting change, but seeking it and focusing on changes you can make on the inside. If you don't try to improve yourself personally every day, you will be stuck in the same place, doing the same things, hoping the same hopes for coming years, but never gaining new territory or winning new victories.

Describe what you believe about your potential. What would you like to be and do? Then describe the changes you need to make to become all you can be.

....
....
....
....
....
....
....
....
....

....
....
....
....
....
....
....
....
....
....
....

DAY

86

*The great mystery isn't that people do things badly
but that they occasionally do a few things well. The only
thing that is universal is incompetence. Strength is always
specific. Nobody ever commented, for example,
that the great violinist Jascha Heifetz probably
couldn't play the trumpet very well.*

PETER DRUCKER

When I first began going after personal growth, I pursued a growth plan that was foundational rather than specific. But as I got older, more experienced, and further in my career, I started to focus my growth in a few key areas. One was communication. That made sense for me, not only because I spoke to audiences four or five times a week, but also because I had some natural ability in that area. Another area was leadership—something I needed to do well every day of my life to succeed in my career.

As you plan your growth, it will benefit you greatly to be focused. In the earlier Daily Dozen decision section on focus, I encouraged you to focus your priorities in three main areas: requirement, return, and reward. You should use the same criteria for your personal growth. *Focus on growing in your areas of greatest strength, not your weaknesses.* And grow in areas that will add value to you personally and professionally.

What are your strengths? What talents, gifts, and skills do you possess? What gives you a sense of life purpose? Write out your thoughts. This is where you want your focus to be.

DAY

87

Love yourself enough to create an environment in your life that is conducive to the nourishment of your personal growth. Allow yourself to let go of the people, thoughts, and situations that poison your well-being.

STEVE MARABOLI

If you've made the decision to pursue growth and experience improvement every day, *learn to enjoy the journey.* If you're going to spend the amount of time learning your career and growing in it, you had better learn to like it. If the destination appeals to you, but you cannot enjoy the journey it takes to get there, you would be wise to reexamine your priorities to make sure you have them right.

And keep in mind that you must *put yourself in a growth environment.* I've often wondered what would have happened if my wife, Margaret, didn't want to grow with me. I wonder because her partnership on the personal growth journey has made all the difference. By working together to improve ourselves, we created a growth environment that helped us to broaden our horizons and live a life that we never imagined when we first got married. If you live in a limiting environment, you will stay small. But if you put yourself in a place that encourages growth, you will expand to reach your potential.

Name your closest associates and whether or not they are hungry to grow and reach their potential. Describe whether your present professional environment is one that fosters growth. What do you need to do to improve your growth environment?

DAY

88

*It's not what we do once in a while that shapes
our lives. It's what we do consistently.*
ANTHONY ROBBINS

Margaret and I did much of our growing together,
but each of us also tailored our growth plans to our individual strengths and needs. One of the results of learning
is that you realize how far you still need to go, and the
more we learned, the hungrier we were for more growth.
I determined to practice this discipline: *Every day I will
grow on purpose with my plan.*

As you embrace the discipline of growth, *make it your
goal to grow in some way every day.* In 1972, an excellent
high school swimmer had the right idea. To make the leap
to become an Olympic-caliber athlete, John Nabor determined to improve by a tenth of a second every month for
the next four years. And it worked. He came home with
five medals, four of them gold. If you want to be successful in your growth, you must desire and plan to improve
a little every day, and you'll make great progress over the
long haul.

What is the next step you will take today to keep moving forward to fulfill the vision for your life?

DAY

89

*If a person will spend one hour a day on the same subject
for five years, that person will be an expert on that subject.*
Earl Nightingale

After I read the Nightingale quote forty years ago,
it changed how I planned my personal growth. I started
spending an hour a day, five days a week, studying leadership. Over time, that practice changed my life.

To make your growth intentional, strategic, and
effective, you need to think it through and plan it well. To
give you an idea, here's how I plan my growth:

- I listen to seven audio lessons every week, trying
  to determine with each what the "take-away" is
  and the one item I can immediately apply.

- I read two books every month, digesting and
  pulling out ideas and thinking about how I can
  apply the concepts to my life.

- I set an appointment every month with someone
  who can help me grow.

As you plan your strategy and set aside time for
growth, don't forget that the more you grow, the more
specific the growth should be to your needs and strengths.
And anytime you discover that a resource doesn't possess
the value you'd hoped for, move on.

Consider your overall plan for personal growth. Write down specific things you will do and the time you will set aside every day to bring it to reality. Commit yourself to following through on it.

DAY

90

*Up is not an easy direction. It defies gravity,
both cultural and magnetic.*
MIKE ABRASHOFF

When you seek and experience improvements daily, your potential grows, and so does your ability to make an impact on your world. To help you do that, *file quotes, stories, and ideas that you find as you learn.* Not only will this habit yield a great harvest of material for your future use, it will also keep you more highly focused, force you to evaluate what you're reading, and help you to go for the good stuff that helps you grow.

Always remember that often the most difficult part of the upward climb of growth is putting into practice what you learn. Yet that is where the true value is. *The final test of any learning is always application.* If what you're learning can be used in some way to help and improve you or others, it is worth the effort. The greatest of all miracles is that we need not be tomorrow what we are today.

Once you have made all the key decisions and each of the twelve disciplines you've worked on for the past eighty-nine days are woven into your life, you'll find that living by your priorities becomes second nature. Soon you'll find that you can make every day your masterpiece.

Take one of the things that you are learning and write a description of how you will apply it to your life over the next week and the compounding benefits that you expect to receive in the future.

The JUMPSTART series by #1 *New York Times* bestselling author John C. Maxwell: 90-day growth guides that will help you become a real success!

Achieve personal and professional success as you explore the five levels of leadership and learn how to master them.

Understand your strengths, identify your goals, and develop habits that will positively impact your future in just three short months.

Become more effective and exceed your own expectations as you discover the eleven types of successful thinking and how to adopt them.

Available from Center Street in print, electronic, and audio formats wherever books are sold.

CENTER
STREET

NEW YORK · BOSTON · NASHVILLE

BE THE LEADER

PEOPLE WANT TO FOLLOW.

▶ JOHN C. MAXWELL

Most leadership training focuses on developing business skills. Our approach is different. We use a transformative approach that emphasizes practical applications.

We at The John Maxwell Company provide comprehensive, practical leadership training and resources that inspire, challenge, and equip individuals and organizations based on the leadership principles John C. Maxwell has taught for more than 40 years.

Let us help you develop and grow your organization's leaders.

800.333.6506
www.johnmaxwell.com

A *Minute* with MAXWELL

Your Free Daily Video Coaching with John

John C. Maxwell's leadership principles are as timeless as they are true. His practical and purpose-driven approach to leadership drives him to live out what he teaches every day. Let John support your success by equipping you with leadership teachings to apply to your life.

Learn and grow every day...

- **Enjoy FREE wisdom & wit** from world renown expert, John Maxwell, on how your success can rise and fall "with every word."

- John will provide you the most **powerful video minute** of coaching on the planet.

- **Benefit** from John's 40+ years as one of the world's top communicators **AT NO COST TO YOU!**

- As a **BONUS**, send John your word, and he will teach on it during one of his videos.

IT'S FREE
Don't Wait!

Visit
www.JohnMaxwellTeam.com/PrioritiesJumpstart
and register today!